COLONIES
OF
PARADISE

COLONIES OF PARADISE

POEMS

MATTHIAS GÖRITZ

Translated by Mary Jo Bang

TriQuarterly Books / Northwestern University Press
Evanston, Illinois

TriQuarterly Books
Northwestern University Press
www.nupress.northwestern.edu

Printed in the United States of America.

10 9 8 7 6 5 4 3 2 1

Library of Congress Cataloging-in-Publication Data

Names: Göritz, Matthias, 1969– author. | Bang, Mary Jo, translator.
Title: Colonies of paradise : poems / Matthias Göritz ; translated from the German by Mary Jo Bang.
Other titles: Loops. English
Description: Evanston, Illinois : TriQuarterly Books/Northwestern University Press, 2023. | Summary: "In Colonies of Paradise, acclaimed poet and translator Mary Jo Bang introduces the poems of contemporary German novelist, poet, and translator Matthias Göritz"— Provided by publisher.
Identifiers: LCCN 2022027453 | ISBN 9780810145818 (paperback) | ISBN 9780810145825 (ebook)
Subjects: BISAC: POETRY / General | POETRY / European / German
Classification: LCC PT2707.O75 L6613 2023 | DDC 831.92—dc23
LC record available at https://lccn.loc.gov/2022027453.

Contents

Room with an Oculus

The Collector: Moscow

Translator's Note

It's difficult to write about childhood—unless, of course, you're Proust. For the rest of us, it's risky. The problem isn't only the need to avoid reductive sentimentality, but also the importance of not overestimating the reader's interest in our long-ago lives when we were each no more than a cutie-pie camera lens taking it all in. In Matthias Göritz's poems, as in *Swann's Way*, childhood is about waiting (will the mother *ever* come and bestow the long-awaited bedtime kiss?). In the world of these poems, however, along with the waiting, there is a constant, low-level sense of menace and a reactive habit of hypervigilance. The result is an eeriness so psychologically rich that it undermines any hint of sentimentality. Göritz also succeeds in this dangerous enterprise by giving his readers just enough narrative to set the scene and then allowing them to fill in the blanks. By not overburdening the poems with particulars, he allows each one to act as a more general template of experience. Readers who are likewise miniaturized by the looming shadow of the past can search their own memories and find parallels.

Göritz doesn't write only about childhood. In these poems, he's also a poet of place, both in the large sense—Paris, Chicago, Hamburg, and Moscow—and in the local sense—the butcher shop, bus station, swimming pool, the suburban hill from which one looks down and sees glass houses. For his speakers, marginality is a way of life; travel only magnifies the sense of remove. Wherever they go, the warily observant children they once were still look out. Those ghost-children aren't the only presences; as in Emily Dickinson's poems, the speaker's inner life merges with objects and landscapes: "The traffic in my head / and the street traffic / tie themselves together" ("The River Running under the River"). Part of the brilliant economy of these poems is that even when they're teetering on the edge of the surreal—as when giant cicadas eye up the speaker in a bar ("Everything Has Been Captured")—they feel undeniably true. Leaving home also allows a degree of freedom that can't be found at home; some of the poems even have an air of exuberant defiance, as if the speaker is reveling in the fact that these are only "colonies" of paradise and not paradise itself, that impossible place of unperturbed perfection supervised by a monocratic father figure: "*I do what I want.* / At night I go alone / through the shadows of the streets" ("Primal Crow").

Göritz is a poet and a novelist, so it's not surprising that a poem can sometimes feel like a fragmented, lyricized, contemporary *Bildungsroman*—a coming-of-age novel that tracks an everyday hero's search for self-knowledge and a sense of tranquility that can't be disrupted by something as simple as downing a glass of milk. Good luck with that, the world says. While slyly gesturing to the genre of fiction, however, the poems also resist narrative structure and timekeeping—there is no "and then this happened, and then this, and then this." They instead move forward via poetry's associative leaps, a strategy that collapses time into a psychological space where a mind leafs through the past while standing at the center of the ever-shifting present.

An interiority this intricate and self-aware creates challenges for a translator. When carrying any text written in one language over into another, one always encounters obstacles—all the more when transporting poems: "The moods, these the words make!" ("The Room"). Metaphor, the brick and mortar of poetry, depends on the exploitation of the multiple meanings inherent in words as well as on the reader's intuitive awareness that for each word, figurative meanings lie in the arms of the literal. In Göritz's poems, the undercurrent of strangeness, along with the sense of narrative abridgement, make it necessary for the translator to take the affective measure of each word and replace it with a word capable of doing the complicated work the original did. What makes this exchange especially challenging is that for all their seriousness, the poems also embody Göritz's distinctively wry sense of humor. The two moods have to be maintained throughout. The irony can't be too strong or the poems will seem insincere; the earnestness can't be overwrought or the poems will seem unmediated. There are also multiple forms of wordplay in the original poems that can't be reproduced in English. Some idioms are unique to a culture; visual puns can't be duplicated. In those instances, I've tried to create wordplay elsewhere while paying special attention to maintaining the same overall balance of intentionality and tone.

Whenever I found it necessary to go beyond a literal word-for-word translation, I tried to stay close enough to the German that a bilingual speaker would easily recognize the original in the translation and possibly even intuit why I had made my decisions. Without that latitude, it would have been impossible to uncover the poems' many covert allusions or tease apart the multiple meanings inherent in the original, often compound, German words. In those moments, I was guided by two things: one, by my understanding of how the poems work—the poetic strategies by which they make meaning—and two, by the need to construct a speaker who may, at different moments, seem either imperturbable or on the cusp of losing control. I was led throughout by Göritz's encouragement to take risks in the translation that would mirror his own linguistic risk-taking in German. In those moments, we were like-minded collaborators. Göritz gave me a copy of his book *Loops* in April of 2016; in the years since, we have met in Berlin, Stuttgart, and St. Louis, and in the ether of email, text, iPhone, and Zoom. His input over those years was crucial to the evolution of these translations.

Poetry is made not only of words and the ideas and visual images they elicit; each poem is a cumulative patterning of language. Sound, rhythm, syntax, punctuation, and line breaks are all manipulated to achieve particular effects. It is the sacred marriage between the totality of those elements and word choice (a polygamy of sorts) that results in the finished poem. Just as we can identify someone we know by their spoken voice, so the ways in which an individual poet patterns language can create a recognizable poetic voice. In poems as intimate and astute as Göritz's, it is essential that the reader not be distracted by the fact that the poem was written in another language. I have tried to create the sense of a speaker who has a consistent voice throughout the poems and who speaks this new language, English, as if he were born to it—that is, with the same fluency and knowledge of craft that the original speaker manifested in German. I tried to match Göritz's sly humor, keen insight, and artistry as I carried over both the contemporary German and the embedded polyphonic echoes of English, French, and Russian into contemporary American English. This book, *Colonies of Paradise*, is the result of those efforts.

COLONIES
OF
PARADISE

Crows

Paris

Primal Crow

The sky
blue above the landscape.
Blue and then the landscape,
the urban landscape.

Crows dangling
like question marks in the breeze.

Trees holding tight,
one sideways glance and they're driven—
into the line of the horizon.
Pillowed on branches,
clouds drag by.

City of metaphors

my day: strolling around
or glances from a window.
Over sterling rooftops,
a still-farther heaven.

Below, in the inner courtyard of a butcher shop,
Jewish, Rue Oberkampf,
over the trashcans a rancid layer of steaming frost.
Smoke break.

The apprentice butcher in his stained tunic
hits a few tennis balls against the brick.

I do what I want.

At night I go alone
through the shadows of the streets.
November

on the Place des Vosges,
at the Canal Saint-Martin
his armored-plated car came by,
winter in it.

Paris is old and cold.

The gray sky, the roof slopes
glittering silver
like frosted leaflets.

In the windows
of the bistros and cafés,
something missing.

Through the city's quiet stillness,
the cold drives me
the throughways, the byways,
from Concorde to Bastille.

You no longer have the Henry Miller line in Clichy.
You no longer have anything other at night anymore.
You can only liken yourself to an unbridled band of diddling birds,

the birds
obscuring the air,
the question marks,
and likewise what seem to be trees,

isolated trees,
with bare limbs,
a shrine of coarse cries.

Second Crow

Day, you
and then the eve of the evening.

From the balcony, sliced light
leaves behind an arm.

Shadow,
in which you for bleeding chrissake put yourself out.

You look through the glossy black,
see into the continual flux,
churning up
inside outside side-to-side:
an effluent running river,
insect-filled,
and one truncated tree—

no square in which to sleep;
you write a brief note.

Change it.

Classic, you think,
as you slide

by means of the motion
deep down in the fingers.

Third Crow

I

Nights.
My legs are empty blanks.
To write about fencing,
and only cover swordplay,

via placating dripped-out baby steps,
with lightning strikes, is like sleep—
that never stops by.

Here they hang. Hands,
like out of bathtubs
and windows. Beckoning with letters.

My legs define the district's limits:
a brimming display case, at the corners, the calico
fringes with their windows, houses, and homes.
Who if not I was living inside?

In there going to pieces:
Everything imaginable: night,
shadows and bogus locked castles.
A mad-dash-brain-race—a dream.

I pull the hem up over me,
this canopy of twenty sleeping sheep,
I sense the gray dread, the dawn, like ice-flowers on frost
bursting into light-based faces and it comes home—

I go
with stepwise progression, to the window,
and decisively slip out

II

We're tangling here
with the heart,

ears listening in
and watching,

as the day
builds itself up from dust motes;

and one, as one

becomes longer,
shadows, on a tree, that break off in a wall.

Fourth Crow

Every ending is . . .
the old beginning
. . . the life that is already evermore so . . .

Scraps of the elders' flipped leaves,
translations from back in the day.
Am I getting carried away by springtime?

I'm up by ten, but it's already just so.
Time ran faster.
Even as I lay me down to sleep,
a lassie's making a mad frantic dash? the old one?
in the red hooded jacket runs past
and sets my beautiful soul on fire.

Here I sit
and as such will become an all day long
Eve.

Able to Imitate

In the beginning was end

Anxiety, of being the machine at the end, a rotting plant, the cerebral mensch getting up in the morning, bending over backwards, just to be in the mirror, like a little sun, hair, face, an ego-I, that persuades itself to be a life, for a fraction of a second. An ongoing boozehound. One that looks at the clock, that says: O, it's time to go. But the O doesn't go. It's sledgehammered, it's on the edge, it sees the high-rise, sees sunrise, which bursts, sees the angel-eye headlights, evening and sunrise, sees people, sees, all views are a review, a case of everything at once, then sees nothing, then (O boy!) everything again, going too far, crashing on the couch at night, then noises in the chamber, where'd it go? It's perched on the wall. What is that, a chamber? Water chamber? It's worse, there are comparisons to be dragged out, my day was very long, how was yours? The echo of the ego inching through the iPhone, the anxiety of being a name at the end, a panther, a man in the gangway, the ordeal, the anxiety of being at the end, and all this as one view, then seen as two, O, one sees it's already three, and again the clock and then the cracked smile, and smiling, just so, without opposition

In the beginning was end

Able to imitate

Fifth Crow

Head rush on the bus, mind-boggle.
I pray for hemoglobin,
I—a moth,
lying on my mouth,
bleeding, like a motherfucker.
On (top of) and offensive in other words.

Here you are, ahead of all,
the crow, craning, you glisten,
and drag, an infinite next,
farther ahead, you see and drag
farther, into a stairwell, a ladder,

a lead-in, to where,
a stairway, up to *pfft!* down the drain,
from story to story,
upward and downward and heartward,

here, you see,
stands my balcony,
waiting while beckoning to
black stones.

The city a silent upright-piano wing.
You see the ravens pull together.
The eyeblink-moment's armada.
You see the eyes tracking.

Light, like the golden giraffe
of good fortune. Slight
in the anthem of your day,
and how terrifying:

head rush, mind-boggle
on the bus, I—lightheaded,
lingo, vertigo.

Disconnect Switch

Viewed from the roof:
light, that

drips from a single incandescent bulb
into the room;

who's that standing in there?
I don't know the face.

Colonies of Paradise

The eyes, rivers and grass—
According to your taste:
the dying off, the dirt.

A house, that bears the imprint of a door, you,
as a wrapped packet in a word chest, the dear sweet boy,
the off that he owns.

And
yet gloriously
empty of language:

You are—a real human being

A crow in the airspace;
You, little man,
are one man—
You are a man, who disbands
and offs your own briefcase
by means of black coffee
or salt
or sunshine.

Lunch break.
Then: off.
One holds off two seconds . . .

then one goes home—to a garden
that is different from the year before last.
One often stands in front of it
as if still waiting around
for something other.

Loops

Chicago

Street Map

The names mean nothing to me
State Street, Clark Street, Belmont
Illusion is not a reliable backup

It leads to the left here
It leads to the right here
from westward toward the east

There is the lake—

But perspiration, of that there's no sign
and of the light between two lucky teeth
that meets with the streets at night

with a slight hollow sound
Here, you think, the overwhelming arrives on its own
I stand at the window and sweat my egocentric I out

Save yourself, who wants to

The River Running under the River

The traffic in my head
and the street traffic
tie themselves together

I hurried down the green hall
to the door
and flipped my bedroom on its head

Hello there? Is it June?
I hid myself
took a trip under my tongue

I thought July? We age
and we change
locally

Chicago, O'Hare
the city the river the lake and the

I thought maybe
a lifetime might be long enough
to buy a pizza pie and even more

to sit in the back seat of a taxi
fixed on a chessboard of streets strapped
into traffic

I thought I am sitting in this city
solid in my body
as if in a rolling chair

Motion made to be motionless

With the steady stream of newspapers
every morning in the omnibus of my little wishes
and evenings with the day's companions

Am I not flitting about?
But, it is just
as if this day didn't even exist

the taste of this particular city
the shadows within it—
the houses all falling down

Perhaps I'm not actually on a trip or only . . .
further, yes, here comes the river again . . .
and here it is again . . . but more . . . under my tongue

During the Day

the high-rises go on becoming
one strung-out

necklace of Lego bricks
a mirror tight with light

block upon block
as if taking a seat

Heaven was there
right beside me

At night
I love the water

especially sweat
while swimming in the lake

I know a sound
(liquid sunshine)

meaning houses-clouding-over-water
everything at the shore

only shadows
on my hand

Night

There where the night broke an arm
on the lamp at the end of the houses
I explain silence

as sound

the tasteful—street flamboyancy
in a mist of atomized kerosene (airfield)—
ends up in an alley

the alley leads
up to the lamp
the lamp

ends
in naught
What is that?
I bring water to a site

That water lacks any taste
First one says airplane
then one says sweat

my entire body soldered
this skin with that water

together
we are emphatic

One is waiting for me

the alley
leads up to the lamp

and ends in

Everything Has Been Captured

The scenery in a photograph
The mood in a script
The major events on the television set

Who still remembers the night of July 30th?
The auburn hair of that owner of a billiard table
mirrored in the flat-screen above the bar

To speak? How bizarre
Those three at the bar are an all-in-one cocktail society
Slowly a ball rolls over yesterday

Was a door slightly ajar?
No, only the sound turned down to near-nothing
Warmth like a sent message

From whom to whom?
We drove from block to block
and up the high-rise house

Below, cars commit
slow-motion acts of self-annihilation
go missing

go faster
go missing
And from somewhere one hears

Flushingsounds
Cicadasong
The glass windowpane pierced

from beneath by a bullet
The landscape lies as in any song

Crouching at the table some touring giant
redeye cicadas
sizing us up
How bizarre we must be made out to be

Cruiser

I would like to put out to sea
Put out to sea I wish to be

my very own frigate
my cabin cruiser

Put out to sea
in a summer full of sweat beads

in the Land of the Lincoln
I know I'm right here

here at a crossroads
State at Grant

turn right off Grant at Wabash
turn right off Wabash at Illinois

and keep turning right off
Illinois at State

Perfected corners
Perpetual spinning top

Could you please cut-and-paste this plot for me
Empty parking lot, little building

the fire lane a darkened canal
my cruiser-I wants to put out to sea

to put out to sea suddenly
go right and right off

The Day after This Day

Daytime
Overnight

The one overview is missing
(Write) it goes backwards

over time

Flat
after the beaten-down karate-chop houses

I'm off to see people living the life
on the edge of the breaking day

Caribou Coffee with moo juice
deep penetrations of sleep

behind the forehead is an error-prone (very mensch-like)
ego-I

Out the door goes
the man with the apple turnover

Sounds as flotsam
While reading is dead in today's paper . . .

I stand up
look at me, I'm off to see

how the city gets itself up

Hallered's House

For Volodya in Moscow

I go to the window
and turn into a beautiful evening

What do you do in heaven?
Whoever dies is no longer in the public sphere

In heaven they dine on ice cream
And if there are dyes?

Isn't color simply the dream of more legroom
I'm in the tummy of Mummy

God makes a perfect pizza there
When I make it out, there's a racket

Mommy is crying
I is crying

Hell, while I really prefer not to imagine it yet
I'm pretty sure it exists

In contrast to a lot of things
nothing is the color white

My mothers all come from monkeys
I can't face a banana anymore

All this makes a ruckus
And purgatory, I assume, is being taken to the cleaners

Everything on earth that is, is dying
And if we go on living, say in heaven

it is raining

Snow

Where the ice trees bloom
winter words tap against the pavement
After the crane world, in comes pigeon world
One can hear their ashy grays scratching at the door

I nodded off in Father's lap
We were counting license plates
40 gas-guzzlers from Germany
10 from measly Bielefeld

Snow
lets its showpieces fall through the darkness
Each snowflake secretly told me its name
Through the windshield I see them charge the glass

A moment ago, it was five
and now it's ten
The fearless captain steers his ship
by the clock

At twelve we have to be in Zurich
It's still a long time to sleep
With a monotone drone we drag our tracks
through that outer space

Oranges in the Window

All penalties are postponed until Wednesday
Snow over everything. Outside rain comes flying in
A soft sound offense. Noises from the window-world
If snow contains the rain?

Gashes and punch-holes in the ground
The fish in the pond stare at the upstairs

Gray garden
A waiting

until summer
comes

Father, Nicki, and Me

My peoplelesson for today
Father, Nicki, and me

Nightly we all hang by threads
No problem, once childhood is

Notably no end
Any who tax themselves at our level become a naught

Table, chair, tight spot, slat
There must be more than that

One day we have a summer
One day we have a spring

We have right now
Right now we have

Played music
That was easy

Father played the flute
Nicki knew to press her finger to a glass

The sound, she says, enters the finger
Once everything has stopped

I put my finger to the glass
Not even summer do have we here

The Room

Squeezed into a corner
furnished with music
At the window the cat watches the fall
moment by moment on the spot

The house open and guests welcome
The driveway full
A look into the garden
I'm out there revealing a secret

Then silence. Someone has just lost his voice
The sounds in the room
hang like billows of smoke
in the geranium bed

The moods, these the words make!

The volunteer mayor of our little town
(word has it he's a Nazi)
makes his cognac flabbergasted
breakup

Even so, Father had a birthday
now he sits checkmated
alone in the armchair

The next few days
he refuses to come with when we go shopping

Flashes

I go
hello lightning strikes

the house
Mother says

you should count
I can't even get to one

Between the needles
at the window's backside

A backup generator
the light goes out

Granddad's been dead for twenty years
but his garden is throwing a fit

It's nice if one knows
where the parents were

flashes. Brighter than any day
Brighter even than those stars

Cathartic Osmotic

Where life exhibits utmost frailty at its outer extreme
Where hard water collects itself
Mornings in the saucepan-teakettle
Mother

Hereupon the disappearing I am
Heated liquid sunshine
Torn by a cloud of two minds

Reviewing the Résumé

Mornings
there's the least resistance

My worker-father
confers with himself
Then the doorbell rings
Then a lightning bolt

The backstabber
happens by

in Daddy's room
the weather is at home
Always ledger-filled
Always smoke-filled

At times one felt
it would be dreadful and meaningful

Of course there's that letter to the father
it says in so many words the tree is already green
he makes our air by taking water and light
and it is something—breathtaking

Won't you come and behold the icy deadness?
You can barely reveal yourself once a day

So Many People Are There during the Day

I sense the moon
as an echo of voices

The dimness

Aching
one night by a thread

I was just thinking what
a cold point   ·

I think about everything
that has happened is happening

Removal

The breath moves in
It brought with it a moving van

Immediately the men with the strong cigar arms arrive
"Did you see that babe in the woods?"

Yep
The theater is empty

I want to sleep
The bogeymen come

and pull the covers down
My left arm dropped off

It's day out there. I'm tired
No one can see me here

"And the little thingies from back in the day?"
"Take 'em away," he says

Yep
After the move-out

The theater is empty

Slowly Things Start to Stay the Same

The air was cold
On bare skin at the side of the pool
Someone lay there and smiled

Unbelievable, said the mother
and meant the dirty smear

At the stop sign, the child walks around his tricycle
The public pool is closed

Outside you can eat the air
Last time I came here

it snowed. The truck rumbled
over the kitten-head cobblestones

The mayor's office still hasn't permitted any heating
The third-floor apartment with the two side-view mirrors at the window

the same woman still lives there
You have to know what's going on around you

I turn around at full speed

The sidewalks now overgrown
The dead landscape behind the pool's wrought-iron fence

the subdivision, the village
to which one drives back

Home, it's called
Home?

I wonder if the paint in the deep end
is still peeling

Craters on moon maps
The water

Blue-green algae
Moldy Styrofoam

Although I wasn't here that often
I'm just looking

The beginning of winter
is a contemptuous time of year

The Suburbs

A mouth-trap snaps over me
Don't worry, it's what's called the sky

At the top of the slope lies glimmering grass
Where are you, man-of-glass

Today he's batting his lashes up there
Heaven on hill on grass

What's going on goes on and on
Behind its backside a dog shits its shit

In the middle upstanding glass
Small house on the outskirts

In this colony I was
for one second long

at home

I Go through the House at Night

In that former house the same shining
white furniture in front of the TV

Time is running
The all-day buzzing vibrates inside the room
The ear inherits

When I saw
the way soldiers smashed a young girl to bits
the pictures crept into my insides

The eye also inherits

In This Neck of the Woods

November. Month of the drowned dog
One sees the lolling tongue drifting along

Quite waterlogged

Relocating the Day

A buy
The sense of: You are here—I am gone

Did I want a hat?
I'm buying the lifestyle

I'm fine with the furniture
I think of them as friends
To the golden sofa
To the shimmery clock

By noon my shadow is hanging by a thread
I grab its hand and yell: Stand up
When I go out I usually forget to bring my hat
Compared to it, the sky is so blue

The moon shines over the city: a short circuit
Then it rains
In the case of the room I'm a glowing timepiece
Tumbling into the green-gold embers of evening
Into the blue whoosh of sleep

Upstairs the TV
Serving a spicy bloodbath
In the first and third programs
News, the day's ruminations
Split segments: limping children
A lonely coffin
And the new heart transplant

In the hall
In coat and hat

Paper Fresh from the Shredder

Wind
then suddenly the trees go crazy
Out goes the one with the ox's head
in comes the one with the cloven hoof

Time flew after the game of chess
In terms of which wind, which rain
You lied
I'm getting sick of it

There are thunderstorms
in which a driving wind takes someone for a ride
I could use a storm like that about now

where time flies by
with wishes and a brimmed hat brought out
under the stars

You say: Thank you, it was a nice time
You took my breath away
It's like I'm clinging to my name
and its letters

Outline

My breath is stopping
The air is tapping
My breath

I was born minus memory
Someone transformed the world
in one spot

running over with music

I Went Out of My Mind

The door has shaken up the house
with me inside it

The sun is shining
A bit much for morning

Afternoon—barely any difference
The house is shaking itself up

the sun
with me inside it

I am
a more unstable border

Horizon
of a world created from last gasps

The day carries them with it
Again and again I feel my tongue in my mouth

The day
The room

The sun
The door

Bonkers
I think to myself

and me inside it

Hallered's House

Slowly
lit from behind

I see the outside through the window
of the car

Trees dressed in morning frost
embracing the house

Glistening grass
The long-legged man with the blue hat

comes out of the house
Take your time. You've prepared yourself

but
you can't take off

After his death

the world will
be different

You listen to the glass
as it crackles in the cold

He turns his face to you
at the very moment

you start
turning the key

in the car

Room with an Oculus

8

Poems head into the blue
      the monster shows

           I am still not
             in the nothing

                 the lovely blank here
               in the blue

                    shows me the monster
                  that says

                I am
                a building seen through

              here at this point:
             a-rising up to

       another more sheer
verse-like here

Displacement

After long drives
the sound effects continue to get together

in the ear
The blood screeches

You keep fishtailing on thin ice
dream-vagabondage, unending

It's morning, then
you see

The sheets line up the leaves on the trees
to give one another hugs

It's a lavish world
In the park you hear the slicing of ice skates

Your face meets the breath
of your shadow

the trees in the woods
In which world can a fish dwell well

Metronome

Imagine that: your ear is not here!
That little tapping of the world—that you hear,
it's rain sinking into the barometer's silence.
The years pass. That means: you are
occupied with something. Time, rhythm, tact as
keeping time. You look at the stars. When you spit
into it, do you sense it: the icy winter morning.
Shoes in the windows before the shop's opening.
Naked lies the light over the shopping mall.
You can sense grass nearby. It's there to hear more
of the world's little tapping. Rain on top of glass.
One step before your door

Strike Out

Around two in the morning it was April

Suddenly I knew
it was pouring

The water barrel stinks
and the spider's hiding

behind the lumber
tomorrow's lurking

the red ball
an oily globe in the grass

Is today
ahead of yesterday?

The neuter that, something-I I call myself
throws a pickaxe over a shoulder

saddles a stylish ballpoint
and heads out the other way

past yesterday
past the day before yesterday
past the day before the day before yesterday
and before!

and at some point, after-as-before,
I forgot about last night
and today, and tomorrow,
this morning

and all the others
that I called days

I am happy

Always give the axe to the close line

Metamorphoses

It is the age of lunchtime
when all the other hours are sleeping
no sleep for you, for now—
is the beginning of this piece of poetry

Heat, a huge stone, lays itself down on the muzzle of a dog,
who is balancing the weight of it
before the butcher shop
into which its owner has zipped

Really, such heat!
when you open the book at Starnbergersee
and see "April is the cruelest . . ." you believe

Ropes of flies droop
inside slice-like display cases
You can see the bellies pulse
and the little hearts beat

It's too hot!
Sound drips
off our foreheads
like clear beads of sweat

Seen through the glass, the glistening
chops

All around you
objects
fall into a trance

It is . . .

your turn
to discover in terms of the sentence
no comment

Room with an Oculus

Hole in the ceiling
the sunlight falls through

Here in the depths you can see
life is nothing but a dream

the passing bus, mirrored in the window
When I was a kid I thought

an earthquake was an orgy
Someone has a hook in my footsy

You know where stories come from
the taken-in in the outback

someone came around this morning
and shoved me under the Styx

On the other side of town
I would have stayed a kid

Off the light
and also out with the cold

Bound

The goalkeeper treasures the moment before his head-butt
four flowers in the window
the stadium bowl still

He thinks
at night in Berlin you can see the picture on the television
flickering in the window

Light-rail rides from Lehnitz to Wannsee
he thinks of his last night at the KitKat (Kazoo-Porn) Club
he thinks

takes the measure of his four cardinal points, then springs up

Late-Afternoon (Delight) Flight

So long the day
yet it's already almost evening

The summer lies
over the landscape
Grassy fields, single houses
Landscape

Still, what's up with living the life?
Puffed up like a monstrous blimp
it moves forward on its forefeet

At noon noises flew through the house
The sounds of lilies
spirit levels, dragonflies
the wind

Someone comes on stage
and says: Come on, let's go into the garden
I'll cut the sky in two
with you

There stands terror in a white dress
A snow-made face
As if in a trance, the flowers seem
to be waiting for me

In this huge transformation of objects
as the sun goes up
the dream-fever heat
goes down

2, 3 Revolutions

Oh you,
who once began
a ballad
with a breezy cakewalk.

You are prudent,
and pleasant, barely hidden
behind the moleskin hedge
just spotted. A brave heart, that

a dog is knocking about.
And over you
a sky that is stretching
its broad face,

when it speaks:
a zeppelin,
a cloud over Alster Lake,
something, that's true,

and you know, it is true;
on the lake,
perhaps one of the boats;

say something,
and you will know
no longer, whether it is true.

We believe in the light.
We believe in you.
We believe in you
for the other.

Still what we believe
will not be,
and what we don't believe
will be

breaking in
to the darkroom
of our minds.

It will develop:
the lonely archaic
friendship and the detachment,
that lets you let loose,

lets loose,

like a thunderbolt,
shooting right through the city,
the rain falling

on all the inconceivable ways
of searching for the means
out of all the mundane,

whatever?
Don't even
minor songs soar aloft?
Songs

without any grand sentiment?
And why shouldn't you
be taken in

to the lit shell
of the shooting gallery
and its owners,

the carnival, and its bliss
sought
in 2, 3 revolutions.

Those who enjoy
circling,
and being?

A human carousel,
filled with chains,
to turn around

and quickly
over and out
cycling, beyond

until the next lamp,
left behind the night.
From afar. Still, the stars.

The Collector

Moscow

Trolleybus No. 3

A hero sets out
in the city to buy, in the wee hours, milk,
traveling by trolley and bus

over
the powdering-gown of traffic,
a white line in a lavender shoe

over
the long boulevard,
the roundabout

past
someone feeding me lines from the city,
Sputnik news

past
past . . . conflicts . . . and beyond those . . .
Abkhazia . . .
more than 107 in the shade . . . the Silverdome . . .
and 5 to 1 . . . the soccer

is still at—
I have never been so far from mastery as now
—when

the *Sport-Express* exits,
a mirror of before
is over   over

the how many lives are there in this fishy business,
in green cock-tails, in green lean-tos,
in the drawn lines of a city?   past

where I am still on the bus?
past . . . And one more question . . . is God? . . .
a relative . . . velocity,

and how far would you . . . go to get away,
to simply sit at the edge of Red Square,
careful not to fall over, and to keep outside
the reach of the machine sweeping the streets

evenings, when more photos still will be made, gradually,
from the things that are there, towers, stone, the light,
and you, as a relative witness, will you turn into a tower,
a yellow dream, a photo, a future distance, that drives you,

to what doesn't yet exist?
past
where a mouth filled with fatigue is gray fur,

into a café,
where you, Mother, your head
never would have stood to be carried

past
and so you are so
over

even a hero
running out of milk
goes out to buy

out there

To Stand

That's the way
an afternoon gets slapped,
together with someone's black hair,
the green fly, dead, the wall, and all,
alongside an afternoon, that dissolves
itself piecemeal, bit by bit,
until it becomes a piece of intel.

There it stands.
Written it stands there.
The till stands. The teller's in-stressed.
People, one by one, in a snaking line,
one asks: "Are you at the end?"
"No, not yet, I'm just one beginning."

Stand still.
I'm also the one who is sometimes that word, and moving myself
more and more slowly ahead and ever onward across all the words.

"Have I become the word made flesh?"—a frenetic back-and-forth,
on a standing-room-only grammarland square.
Stand up.

The red air falls away.
The rain outside. Umbrellas and screens converge.
Faces in the glass square.
If we are We it is only because we are herein in the rain
standing by,
one Here, as usual worth less than a red cent: Precisely!

Let the record show:
That Here.
That big-box GUM store.
The day—a Today—15—therein in May.

The day spent with.
The exchange rate (deviation index).
The big-box store detective.

Where To

that language,
translatable into stone blocks for building,

Russian, the gazillion ways of zipping about,
and still the street not found: Walk on into

In-Between:

Maybe it's only silence crouched there.

Everyone's suspended in their thoughts,
a dirty dozen ego-I's,
naked bent-back thoughts.
TV-time's nape of the neck,

the switchblade road into the blue.
I have not yet met a single self.
What's going on in your mouth? Propositions are,
your ears are getting a bellyful, your hands go on decomposing

on you, and what did you come here to do?,
the same here, the yellow smell,
a pair of languages, a pair of loafers, and we,
the lexical pairing—

The hands are closed, a sign hangs on your hide:
Honestly, description is the best policy.

Anyway, A is Epidermis. Outer rim of the human, the plant family,
the animals, cuticle, large-pored by comparison,
a varied coat of many colors.

Where does the skin end and this skin from that skin.
Where does the human begin.

Where does the word.
Where you.
Where to.

My Iceberg

                                    And if you ever could
                              discover a word,
                         it would be false,
                    and also inadequate.

It stands,
I grant you:
in a church,
on any given day.
The light is white—from the standing candle, it's there,
where a hand swings incense in a censer, and there's singing and one and all
stands in

for any and all,
one song, and behind the gold leaf
on the altar   is God?

Is that
singing coming from those mouths?
Are there: faces behind the beards,
the black caps going back and forth in the belief before them,
as—if there's another you other than me,
that speaks,
my   wishes.

So it stands,
always more and more, a blank slate—
as a sign?   There's nothing to see.
I see the arm of a white-haired woman
turning into a candle.
Let there be light!

In this red-gold world
I can't make any sense. I want out.

My mass
is Heisenberg,
who speaks of the relative, observing I.
I am at home in that era, in this skin,
a visitor, visionary, there, where place solves for point of view,
no one pledging before and after
where all truth is a known conspiracy, no me and no you
and no one infallible word to stand in for the
actual

Maschina Vremini

the firm wet fog—
this black anthracite of night
in the red cycle of a city

        Where you—
        there was an earlier
        one

and was
an even later one
of afore, ago

        fore- and fore- and fro!
        and before and before and before
        and before—wherebefore

should I
wherefore
still going there?

        and stop! makes
        one
        where you

still are
a silent day
and nothing is noisy

        I'll give it all up
        what stops
        you and me

And I know how to play snow, white
(there was one before!)
was!

so what ?
so what ?
and one

the ebony, hair—
the time was there
and then swam on or off again

That Time Machine

Morning

Under a canopy sky,
a man settles down,
a plastic apron on.

As the train slips away
evenly, a ghost is left back on the tracks,
I open the window,

glance into the courtyard
at the statue of Kirov.
The Marshal as usual is raising his hand:
Greetings, People
Hello, Hello, fellow Communist Party members.

The pigeons shitting on it
belong to this land,
not to the hand that is hiding
the clouds with its greeting,

while flies attack a fruit stand,
and melons spill from a pile,
and armor-plated bursts
flash from the hill here,

the sun is rising,
and at the other window,
there's a sound
settling over that land.

A new, nearly red sound.
It flies in through the window.

Throughway

Faces, facing one another on the bus.
A batch of egos gathered by chance,
elemental weather or work hours.

Call it: a bus, a driving apparatus,
or simply: a frozen-over association.
Is that the vague question of the day? How do we see ourselves?

Out there, seeable with the naked eye, snow lies.
Like road recyclers, the drivers make tracks,
which then, as they leave one realm,
appear in another, then in the nearest next.

We—the snow's honored guests—
touch down here, at a stop in the East,
in a quarter-precinct that stands for the whole.
Denizens of a diminutive continent,

robbed of our breath,
by riding on a bus,
or at the hands of the cold.

Just this once, we see
how it is, to be arriving as one in a crowd,
through the eyes of the same,
through the eyes of the others.

Russian Milk

I rinse out a glass.
Was milk.

The daily arming for war.
To stand up for a day.

To put oneself down at night.
What occurs when one stays up?

What happens when you lie?
Diddly-squat.

Really nothing?
I rinse out a glass.

Was milk.
Will be milk.

Tomorrow around this time.
If I'm hungry

and thirsty.

My Head Expands

I've looked too deeply into the glass,
which works like a telescope.
The tadpole head is held up
by the cockroach at the stove's edge.
She peers at me
as she drags her pregnant belly
into the icebox underworld.

So, I say,
when the door bursts open,
I see inside it's also winter.

What am I missing?
I have a place,
a bit of money
and a window.

My elongated brain drives through the day,
equipped with my eye,
outfitted in my body,
addressed by me,
it gathers impressions.

Where is it going?
The transport mediums are
the modes of transport: feet, legs, auto, and bus.
Every day I see people
vanish through the subway entrance,
that atom smasher for the human masses.

Sometimes I'm also in there,
always coming in, late
even faster,
to the job,

to the agreed-upon date,
back to the desk.
I can hardly bear to say so, but
sometimes I think
it's all a game my mind made up.

I've looked too deeply into the glass.

It is all crystal clear
you don't go up against the day.
I've made a place for myself,
a bit of money,
and take a stand at the window.
Outside goes on.

Traffic flow.
Life flow.
Nightfall.
The entrances and exits,
the whole theatrical to-do.

Red Series 52

What's left of me
other than an ego-I,
one erected right here
in our Mighty Fortress:
Language is not God
and I keep it freely
prostitutable—pronominal;

however, Friday's brief daylight rain has the nice silence
of a blue Aral AG filling station, where I can
rest myself in these words for a spell.
Have you slept through the end?

One
What is so bad about a number? Three-fourths you,
I one-twenty-five, the half, past . . . twelve . . . o'clock,
at night, and so on until the red sky of sunrise—

there could be worse beginnings, the abrupt middle-of-the-night
wake-up and just-get-up, let yourself take the umbrella

that's been left, leave by way of the third-floor steps
to the second, to the first—and you're out—

you, in the naked dark gray, under Tarkovsky's rimless sky,
where one can quickly rope-climb rain-threads,

and there one can see: night
and can breathe

and one only need open the umbrella
and one can fly

and be a dandelion dressed in black
and can be called Jakob, or Robert

it doesn't matter,
it doesn't matter!

and see from on high what's going on down on earth
and possibly see on the street a single, slightly odd, woman

and the single, slightly odd, woman says "Hi!"
and if the one also says "Hi!" and if one is all smiles one is already all wet

and moves quickly off and hears whistling in the wind
and the streetlights below and the sense of a heart,

and all is so vast and beautifully electric
and thrilling, that one can't actually hold back bliss,

and then one flies off elsewhere, where one can sense grass,
and lands on one's feet, and everything smacks of see-through chives,

and under dripping trees one excitedly breaks open one's mouth
and morning comes roaring in "two!", "three!"

and   "fifty-two!"
and laughs

and the umbrella-screen has been folded over
            "one-half!"

and it could go on like this forever
            "two!", "three!"

Robert Jakob Maria Marina Luisa
and fifty-two

and four
and you,

some one, and me too.

In the Casing of Time

It's incredibly deep, people's sleep
inside the downpourmachine

noises
from the insides of time

from the organ works
elongated tones emerge

the outstanding radial tire
tracks, traffic

circles carried on
from the morning

the colors are commutable
the driver's license names

get slipped into the morning
from that sleep

like a pneumatic tube
into the city's bloodstream

go with the flow
or keep sleeping

gray are the innards of the ticker
sleepless and deep

lies its meat
in the casing of time

Lesson

Nearly all alone
one came down to the other.
I had laid down.

Poetry
glowed like a bright tab
of aspirin under the skullcap.

How seeable was the barely sayable!
Like a picture by Kandinsky
that ran upside down through the room,
lines were being spouted from the treetop,
without missing a beat, Dostoyevsky
carried the bathrobe from room to room
when I like said to him: "Hey, Fyodor, just *wear* it . . ."

So it goes
but not every time,
if you believe you can correctly measure your hide
using the atlases of biology
and language theory,
or if you are overconfident
holed up as you are in your metaphorical castle-keep.

I've seen a lot
in these gardens and in those museums,
in these museum gardens, those garden museums,
and a fair bit in the street,

just as much
as when seeing what I've seen
in the gardens, the streets, the rooms.
I stretched myself out.

More than one mere tab of aspirin,
the way eyeballs roll back,
like the eyes of sports cars when sleeping.

That's the way it goes.
Almost on its own
the poem
ran into me.

The Collector

And Moscow's on fire, all's in—one and all—
the Kremlin cupola glistens in the light.
The fog rolls on, a worn gray man in a hat,
night backpedals into the subway shafts.

The waxen faces—dreamers—get off,
the day begins—a big gray racket—
at one point on Manege Square,
a yellow Cat rips up the street,

"Is Lenin still asleep?"

and red are the museum bricks under the silver roof,
and yellow—barracks walls, where later faces will hangdog
high above the Unknown Soldier's flame,
which was wide-awake burning again last night.

The morning air soon won't keep quiet.
The birds flee, alone the gray-black ravens
rule over the asphalt, hold your hounds up!
In the sky, the brief bark of the first thunderstorm—

"Is Lenin still asleep?"

Not yet! The sun is already getting started.
In Alexander Garden the first women are dragging
the white carts, hot sausages, ices, pierogies, juice,
maybe an old man is still sitting on a sagging bench

wearing his life and the olden days as medals.
One can see far more clearly now. The anglers below
on the dead river, so good at keeping quiet
in the run-amok traffic, the machines, a bit further up, they

"And Lenin? . . ."

sit there, as silent as never on no day till now. Perhaps
now is the time for clearing the mind. For a long while
the day floats alongside me, I pick up and gather in
everything, whatever glistens in light—since I'm a collector,

and like a sonar generator the clock pings out the hour,
the big circular world sinks on Red Square,
and Lenin sleeps, and I—a big ear—hear and stop
everything, take it all in, and Moscow's on fire, it glistens,
am I on my own?,

the light breaks off.

Acknowledgments

Thanks to the editors of the following magazines where the translations in this collection, sometimes in earlier versions, were published.

The Believer (online), October 28, 2019: "Reviewing the Résumé"

Bennington Review, no. 9 (2021): "So Many People Are There During the Day" "2, 3 Revolutions"

Columbia Journal, no. 58 (2020): "8," "Outline," "Red Series 52," and "Slowly Things Start to Stay the Same"

Conjunctions (online), September 19, 2017: "Everything Has Been Captured [as 'Everything is captured']," "Night," "Primal Crow," and "Street Map"

Crazyhorse, no. 97 (Spring 2020): "Able to Imitate" and "Late Afternoon (Delight) Flight"

Exchanges: Journal of Literary Translation (Fall 2019): "Father, Nicki and Me," "Flashes," "Lesson," "Oranges in the Window," "The Room," "Room with an Oculus," and "Snow" (a brief "Translator's Note" accompanied these poems; some of the language from that note appears in the longer "Translator's Note" at the front of this book)

Gulf Coast, 31, no. 2 (Summer/Fall 2019): "Colonies of Paradise"

Harvard Review (online), April 30, 2020: "I Went Out of My Mind," "Metronome," and "Third Crow"

Iowa Review, 50, no. 1 (Spring 2020): "To Stand" and "Trolleybus No. 3"

jubilat, no. 38 (2020): "Cruiser," "During the Day," "Paper Fresh from the Shredder," and "The River Running Under the River"

The New Republic, September 25, 2020: "Morning"

Plume (online), December 18, 2019: "Throughway"

Poetry Magazine, 215, no. 4 (January 2020): "Fifth Crow" and "Second Crow"

A Public Space, no. 29 (2020): "In the Casing of Time" and "My Head Expands"

Puerto del Sol, no. 56 (Fall 2021): "Displacement," "Metamorphosis," and "Osmotic Cathartic," and "The Suburbs"

Smartish Pace, no. 27 (April 2020): "Disconnect Switch," "Hallered's House," and "Relocating the Day"

TriQuarterly, no. 158 (Summer/Fall 2020): "My Iceberg" and "Where To"

Tupelo Quarterly (online), March 14, 2020: "For Volodya in Moscow," "In This Neck of the Woods," "*Maschina Vremini*," "Removal," and "Russian Milk [as 'Downy']"

Yale Review (online), May 12, 2020: "The Day after This Day"

Thanks to Ilya Kaminsky for awarding the poem "Colonies of Paradise" a 2018 Gulf Coast Prize in Translation. Thanks to Henrik Drescher for the generous use of his painting *Distractor* for the cover. Thanks to Ervin Malakaj for his very patient German lessons and for introducing me to Matthias Göritz in 2014. Thanks also to my sister, Norma Jean Endersby, and to friends as near as my neighborhood and as far away as Tokyo. Boundless gratitude to Marisa Siegel at Northwestern University Press for her confidence in and enthusiasm for this book, and to everyone at the press who assisted in bringing it into the world. To Matthias Göritz, thank you, thank you, thank you, for your wonderful poems, and for trusting me with them—and for the countless conversations about how to make them act in English as they act *auf Deutsch*.